A Boy from Porbandar.

The Childhood Stories of Mahatma Gandhi

Briji. KT

Ukiyoto Publishing

Preface

A soulful story.

The early life of Gandhi is mostly unknown. Schools focus on the end of his life, and his act as a freedom fighter. But hardly anyone talks about Gandhi as a child. But this book rises above the rest, shedding light onto his childhood. From stories of schooldays, to his vow never to lie, Briji KT's new book stretches across his life. It begins at Gandhi's childhood, when he was not the one and only Mahatma Gandhi, but instead little Mohandas. His childhood is brought to life by Briji's expressive word choice and style. Her story-like fact book is sure to be a giant hit for kids, for it is fun, yet factual.

Briji Kt put a million years' worth of effort into this, resulting in a story beyond the limits of a usual history. It's like an exquisite painting. You can practically feel Mohandas's sadness when he admits of stealing to his father, and relate to him as he grows up. The book sucks you into the story, and you end up enraptured in it, going through the ups and downs of Gandhi's life.

When he grows up, his troubles with racism are portrayed clearly. Briji KT showed the darkness he undertook in a breath-taking way. His attempts in a court are as crystal clear as a river, and when he finally dies, the words 'Hey Ram' send the readers to tears.

As a friend of her, I am very honored to write the forward of such a great book. Words cannot portray it, for it is more than that. This book is a great picture of Gandhi's life, and will be a sure favorite of everyone who reads it.

- Austin Ajit

Austin Ajit

I'm an eleven-year-old child from Bengaluru studying in grade 7 at Wolsey Hall Oxford, the home-schooling, UK. I wrote three fiction, one short story collection one non fiction and four translation books.

I have had a deep passion for animals and nature, ever since I was small. I love learning and writing about new, uncommon animals (like Okapi, Purple frogs, Manned wolves, etc) and enjoy learning about the different creatures that live in our world! I like spending time in forests and green places, and like gardening.I spend my free time reading, drawing, and exploring my backyard for insects and other creatures.

I spread the message to save nature through my books, which I publish to spread awareness on our earth's situation. Whatever I earn from these books goes to sponsor a sick sloth bear named 'Kuber' in wildlife SOS's Bannerghatta sanctuary. I hope that more people stop and save nature and its inhabitants, before it's too late for us, and the natural world.

When I grow up, I want to be a naturalist or paleontologist.

Apart from reading and writing, I love drawing and experimenting in various mediums like pencil, pen, crayons, acrylic and oil pastels. I also love travelling to discover new places, trekking, wildlife safaris and bird watching.

To my dearest Evaan.

AUTHOR'S NOTE

The life of Mahatma Gandhi, the Father of our nation is written in every language. His struggle and sacrifice during the freedom movement for the independence of India is venerable. He was also the leader of the freedom struggle of Indians in South Africa.

This book, covering a few childhood stories of Gandhiji is to enlighten the present day children to know how an ordinary boy turned out to be a 'Mahatma'!.

Gandhiji, the average school student neither showed extraordinary ability in anything nor gave any expectation to become a great leader.

Later he was the one who led our country to freedom with his weapon of non violence and brought the British to its knees!

Gandhiji said that, the future of a country lies in the hands of children, and this book is dedicated to the modern day children who are fortunate enough to be born in a free India. Gandhiji loved children and he was 'Bapu' for them. He dreamt for a country where all children must get education which is the basic right of them.

This book is a humble attempt to urge children to know our heritage. Wherever you are in the world, you must be proud of being an Indian. For this, one must know about the leaders who lived and died for India, as Indians . There were kings and warriors who fought against British, starting from 'Maveeran Alagumuthu Kone, Mangal Pande, Rani

Lakshmi Bhai,Pazhasi Raja,Tipu Sultan, and many more who became martyrs in action!

[The British East India company came to India as traders of spices, a very important commodity in Europe back then.As the kings of small provinces were divided for and against East India company, the British took advantage of the situation. They manufactured everything locally by making people work like slaves for no wages and sold in the world market. They looted the whole country.]

The Indian national army founded by Subash Chandra Boss,and extremists like Bhagat Sing were aggressively active in the freedom fight during that time with a different view and extremist ideas to tackle the Empire. But Gandhiji's ideals and principles found victory where all other methods were failed. His principles were based on truth.

 All children must read the autobiography of Gandhiji "The story of My experiments with Truth,

 Gandhiji said " A man is but the product of his thoughts. "

Children must grow up into people of ideals and principles based on truth. Leave a bench mark that "I lived here ' and your life must be worthwhile and for a good cause .

You shall be remembered for ever!

Contents

Chapter - 1: A Boy From Porbandar

"A man is but the product of his thoughts. What he thinks he becomes."

-Mahatma Gandhi

The name Mahatma Gandhi is revered by all Indians as he is the Father of our nation.He dedicated and sacrificed his life for the freedom which we enjoy today. Todays' children may not understand the real value of freedom as they are born in a free country.

Our country was under British rule, whose vast empire expanded several territories all over the world after every war. "The sun never sets in British Empire!" became an unchallenged title given to that country as they have captured territories in all directions!

British occupied Indian territory by defeating all regional kings and queens who were martyred.They ruled us around Eighty nine years and it was Gandhiji who disarmed them without blood shed ,but with his principle of Ahimsa and non-cooperation which won our freedom in 1947. Gandhiji was honoured and given the title "Mahatma" by the world famous poet and freedom fighter Rabindra Nath Tagore.

Gandhiji who was so fond of children believed that the future of a country is in the hands of children. Children called him Bapuji lovingly.

The name "Bapuji", especially in children's mind brings a picture of an old man with a round framed specks who laughs innocently with no teeth in the mouth!

Little they know that the same old man and the Father of our nation also had a childhood like any other child.

Gandhiji was born in a place called Porbandar situated in western coastal region of India on October 2nd 1869. He was born in a dark room which had no windows in the downstairs of a white washed house. The wheatish boy was an average looking normal child with a very small physique.

His birth was one among the several common birth in India. His Father was Karamchand Gandhi and mother was Putlibai Gandhi. Putlibai was Karamchand Gandhi's fourth wife as all three previous wives had passed away by illness.

The child was named "Mohandas Karamchand Gandhi "after the Family name and father's name.

His grand Father Uthamchand Gandhi was very intelligent though he was from a common trader's Family. He excelled in governance and he was very popular among the people. Thus he became the

'Diwan ' of Porbandar state of British India. "Diwan" can be explained as the Chief minister of a state.

Mohan das 's father Karamchand Gandhi also had excellent knowledge and wisdom in administrative strategy. He was very courageous also. He held the position of Diwan of Porbandar and Rajkot respectively.

As the youngest in the family Mohandas was loved and pampered by everyone. He was addressed as ' Moniyya 'lovingly. Mohandas loved his mother who was always spending time in ritual fasting and prayers rather than the short tempered father!

As many of you children, Moniyya dreaded darkness .It may be symbolic to his birth in a very dark room, darkness haunted him always. Those days there was no electricity and the darkness was so terrible that he explains the pitch darkness as total blindness. He was not able to see even his palm from a very close range!

It was a nightmare for Moniyya to go from one room to another when it becomes dark after sun set.

When he tries to look at the dark room itself he see all sorts of serpents and snakes sway fiercely and ghosts move menacingly in the spooky room. He was so scared to think straight and wisely as he was a small child.

One day he was playing outside and never noticed that it became dark after sunset.Though there may be a little brightness outside after sunset, it will be pitch darkness inside the house as there were no big windows for the house.

He looked around in fear. There were no body outside. He had to go either to the room or climb upstairs to look for his mother. When he tried looking in the corridor,serpents were charging at him with vengeance. Blood thirsty Ghosts were appearing here and there. He was scared to death and closed his eyes. He was shivering with fear.

Suddenly he heard a voice and frightened. His heart raised and mouth went dry.

"What happened little masterji ?"Heard a voice.

Moniyya left a sigh of relief. That was their maid Rambha. She came with a lantern.

"Are you afraid?"

Moniyya took time to answer as his mouth was dry because of fear.

"Yes…! Yes Dhayee.I am scared."

" Okay. Tell me one thing. What was that you scared of?"

He looked around and said in a low voice.

"There are snakes and serpents all over. I saw ghosts also."

Maid Rambha laughed.

"There is nothing here. Take a look properly. I would like to tell you something. Do you know there is somebody who does not have any fear for all these serpents and ghosts."

"Who is that?"

Moniyya was fascinated to know about that hero.

"Lord Sri Ram!!" She said.

"Whenever you get scared just call him immediately. Sri Ram will come and get rid of your fear."

"Will he come even if I call? " Moniyya was doubt full.

"Yes. Of course. Rambha assured him. Sri Ram likes children better. Take him along where ever you go. Then there is no need to be scared of anything."

After that, Moniyya learned to chant the prayer of Ram.

He realised that this practice of chanting the name of Ram boosted his self confidence and courage to face anything. He decided not to be afraid of anything after that.

When Gandhiji was gunned down by a religious extremist Nathuram Godse he fell chanting the name of Ram. He left his life by uttering the name.

"HEY RAM"!!

Chapter - 2: The Trustworthy Moniyya

"A coward is incapable of exhibiting love., it is the prerogative of the brave."

- Mahatma Gandhi

Mohandas's Father Karamchand Gandhi alias Kaba Gandhi served as Diwan of Porbandar and Rajkot under British rule. He was a very courageous personality who dare to salute the Nawab of Junagadh with left hand.

He said boldly that "my right hand is for Porbandar."!

Moniyya was so scared of his father who bore positions of the highest order.

His mother Putlibai was a kind hearted soul who always attended the sick in the family and spent her time in prayers and rituals. She was very intelligent and bold as well.

Mohandas had observed people approaching her for her advice in many matters.

She will always keep vows for different needs and the day she worships Sun God,she will fast until the sun appears in the sky!

 In winter season,some days,the sun cannot be seen as the clouds cover the sun. Mohandas will gape at the sky constantly to see the sun. The moment when the Sun appears he will run to bring his mother to see it and break her fast. But, by the time he brings his mother the clouds cover the sun and it disappears.

Mohandas use to feel bad for his mother who is fasting until the sun appears. Mohan das considered his mother as a Holy lady.

At the same time Mohan Das had his own independent opinion and he never hesitated to express that.

His mother use to tell a lot of stories and he grew up listening to those moral stories. Out of many, the story of Sravan Kumar fascinated him so much because the small boy had dedicated his life to look after his blind parents.

The story goes like this.

"Sravan Kumar was the only son of his parents who are blind. He looked after them very well by meeting all the needs as they need help even for their daily routine

One day Sravan Kumar decided to fulfil the wish of his blind parents to go on a pilgrimage. Those days there were no motor vehicles. Normally all journeys were by foot for common people. It was so difficult to take both of them by foot as they were blind and old. Sravan made two big baskets and tied on both the sides of a long wooden log like a balance. He made them sit in the basket and carried them placing the log on his shoulder.

At one place in the wilderness, his parents requested him to put them down as they were very thirsty. Sravan went in search of water and happened to see one river. He took a mud pot and dipped to fetch water from the river. At the same time King Dasratha was out hunting in the same forest. He heard the noise of Sravan filling water in the pot,and mistook it for an elephant .He shot arrows to the spot which killed the boy!

The story continues as the repentant King Dasaratha brought water as well as Sravan's body to the old blind parents. Without realising who the man was,they cursed him to face the same fate as them. They said.

"You will also die a lonely death without your children around for your last rites."

Mohan Das decided to serve his parents as Sravan.

At times Mohan Das felt very low as he was bullied and beaten up by friends and even by his own brother. He felt very inferior and hopeless that he was dark with a small physique. He had no confidence to counter them or stand in front of them. He use to run back home crying.

Watching him cry,his mother use to scold him for not being bold enough to stand up for himself. She said.

"You must be bold enough to defend yourself. Return the blow and protect yourself. If you are timid and give them a chance to think that you have no confidence in you, they will take advantage and defeat and bully you always."

Then,suddenly Mohan Das will change his attitude and prove that his mother was wrong. He said.

"Why should I beat my brother. It is wrong.We must pardon those who do wrong things."

Putlibai shook her head in surprise and said to herself.

"I wonder who is putting such ideas in his head ".

Those days the discrimination based on cast and creed was at its peak. People were divided due to these practices. Cast system was prevalent and Hindus followed the cast system with the observance of heredity in occupations and marriage.They observed untouchability towards the low cast people those who were at the service of the high cast.

One day Mohan Das got some sweets and he went and gave to 'Ukka 'the son of his servant who was a low cast untouchable.

Ukka was surprised and scared and stepped back. He said.

"Little master,I am an untouchable. If you touch me you will become impure. " Mohan Das laughed.

"How will I become impure if I touch you. "

Mohandas stepped forward and put his arm around him and gave him the sweets.

" I want to become your friend."

Putlibai saw this and was very furious. She warned Mohandas.

"We are high cast Hindus and he is an untouchable low cast. Never touch him again!"

"He is also a human being like me. How will I become impure If I touch him. "Mohandas questioned his mother.

Putlibai became very angry and said.

"Don't teach me. Go and take bath immediately and ask pardon to God before entering the house!!"

Then, in the course of time Gandhiji worked hard for the upliftment of these untouchables and earned them an equal status in the society. He started many programmes to bring them to the main stream and urged the society to shed all the discrimination of upper or lower cast. Gandhiji named them "Harijan" which means beloveds of God.!

Once, Mohandas had been to a famous play "Sathya Harishchandra" in which a King was tested by Gods but he never failed to uphold truth. Mohan Das liked the play and he was pensive.

 In the play,King Harishchandra faced several disasters in life but never left the path of truth. He had to sacrifice everything and even the kingdom. He ended up as an undertaker in a crematorium . He happened to see his wife who was once the queen,brought his dead son for cremation. The heart broken king,by hiding his tears,asked the lady to give the charges for cremation which she failed to give.

The lady never recognised her husband the king,who was in the attire of an undertaker who cremate bodies. Though the terrible and unbearable testing will tempt any body to leave the path of truth, the king over comes all the dilemma in life and never left the path of truth.

Mahatma Gandhiji referred this story in his autobiography "My experiments with Truth."

From his childhood he never faulted on truth. He has quoted an incident he experienced in his school as an example for this.

When Mohan Das was seven years old, his father Karamchand Gandhi became the Diwan of Rajkot. So Mohandas was admitted to a school in Rajkot.

According to the young Mohandas, shifting from his birth place in Porbandar to Rajkot was heartrending.Porbandar was a beautiful harbour which was facing the Barda hills. He love to watch ships moving in the deep blue ocean.

When he came to Rajkot he miserably missed the port,ships and the deep blue water. He felt like crying in the memories of his grandfather's house where he was born.

Mohandas was an average student. He didn't excel in studies. But he was very hardworking. He never tried any alternative method or short cuts to avail more marks or to impress teachers to earn appreciation. He never lied in any circumstances .

One day the education officer Mr Giles came to the school for inspection.

In fact this inspection is carried out to check the efficiency of teachers in teaching. The education officer will come to every class and either direct the teacher to teach or ask question to the students directly. He will assess the standard of the children and the efficiency of the teacher.

These inspections are nightmares for both the children as well as the teachers.

During the course of inspection, Mr Giles reached Mohandas's class. It was English period and the officer asked the teacher to take a dictation of English spellings.

There was pin drop silence and the teacher started dictating English words. He called out five words and Mohan das was doubtful about one word "kettle". He wrote only one 't' for kettle. The teacher noticed him writing only one 't', he gestured him that it was wrong. He silently intimated him to look at the student next to him and write correctly.

When the teacher realised that Mohandas was not noticing his attempts to show that he was wrong, he came near him and kicked him softly with his boot and showed him the other student's book.

But Mohandas didn't look at the other student's book and kept on wondering about the strange behaviour of the teacher. A teacher who was expected to lead students in the path of truth and honesty forces him to malpractice!!

After dictation, when the Teacher checked all the books,Mohan das was the only one student made the mistake and his teacher became furious. Though Mohan das felt bad that Teacher was upset only because him, Mohandas was happy inside. He overcame all the temptations and instructions to copy but he never copied. In 1880 Mohan Das was admitted to Alfred high school in Rajkot.

Chapter - 3: Alfred School Alias Mohandas Gandhi School

"Live as there is no tomorrow .Earn knowledge as we will never die."

– Mahatma Gandhi

Mohan Das Gandhi has the distinguished honour of changing a school's name itself in his name! Alfred school became "Mohan Das Gandhi school."

Political Agent Mr. Karnal Singh built the first ever English Medium school in Saurashtra. The school which started in 1853 October 17th was known as Rajkot high school in the beginning. The school was completed and started functioning in the year of 1868

Later, Nawab ' Sir.Muhamad Bahadur Khanji Babi 'constructed it further and gave the name Alfred School in the memory of Edinburgh Duke Prince Alfred. In 1875 Bombay Governor Sir Philip woodhouse inaugurated the school.

In 1881 Mohan Das was admitted to Alfred School. It is said that Mohan Das was an introvert at that time.

He use to hurry home as soon as the school gets over. He never showed any interest in making friends and spending time with them. He was a boy of few words and unlike other children he never was interested in making friends and playing with them.

He had spent most of the time inside his room, reading. A kind of inferiority complex was haunting him. Though he didn't express his feelings, he was mentally disturbed and depressed. He looked at other class mates who were all tall, good looking and smart. He thought that he was not as good looking as them nor he is of average size to be with them. He was dark, frail and short!

He didn't know to rise up to their standards who boost themselves and were very proud. Mohan Das was not a bright student also. He never showed any interest in extracurricular activities or sports. He has written about this in his autobiography. He will be surprised if and when he receive a scholarship or Medal!

But he was a hard working student. He never gave up. He was a fighter.

The medium of Education was English and that itself was a huge challenge for him. More over he was not in the opinion of byhearting everything without any basis or logic.

He liked Geometry out of all subjects. It is because,in Geometry you can prove it logically based on a reason. It is a science which can be proved practically.

Mathematics and Algebra were very difficult and Mohan Das dreaded Sanskrit period.!

Then a teacher named Krishna Sankar Pandya explained that it is the language of Vedas and must be learned with due respect. Mohan Das worked very hard and somehow he managed to become little familiar with the Language and studied hard.

He has no respect to his class mates who scored more marks through byhearting the lessons.

Mohan Das believed in wisdom and knowledge based education,rather than mug up without understanding the core idea. He never believed and supported examination. Examination must not be a measuring scale among students and it is wrong to assess and examine who is cleverer than whom.

Later,with all these ideas, Gandhi started his dream school when he was fighting for the freedom of Indians in South Africa. He started two Ashrams for community living in South Africa. Phoenix settlement in Durban and Tolstoy farm in Johannesburg. This was meant for training and preparing people for non-violent Sathyagraha.

Phoenix was the place Gandhiji started his school based on his ideas and principles. He appreciated children those who scored less mark rather than students who scored high marks by byhearting! He shared his own study experience when he was in School.

Examination should not be a practice to assess who is cleverer than whom. It must be for taking a stock of the improvement achieved by that student in his academics. Tests must be given only to check how much improvement the student achieved from the previous performance.

A bright student should not compete with a weak student because eventually he will become lazy, thinking that he is more intelligent. This overconfidence will make them lethargic and quit hard working.

When Mohan Das was studying in Alfred School, he had undergone some changes in behaviour and it was a testing time for him as all teen agers. Almost all teenagers will go through this rush of emotions ahead of consciousness and understanding, They may fall for all kind of temptations during this period .

Mohan Das had few friends and he always was in the company of his elder brother. Brother's close friend one Sheik Mehathab befriended Gandhi during these period. Gandhi admired him for his personality as he was very good looking and healthy.

As Gandhi was afraid of everything this boy was a dare devil. He was not afraid of anything and dare to hold snake and lizards in his hands. More over unlike Gandhi he was not afraid of ghosts!!

He had noticed that even his wife Kasturba also was not afraid of anything. On the other hand Gandhi was scared of everything. He wanted to be adventurous and brave but he could not.

He felt so inferior and hopeless. He was neither grown up into a man, nor a child to be afraid of everything.

Sheik Mehtab came up with a new discovery that people who ate non vegetarian food had more strength and beauty. He said.

"Look at the British. They are huge and very good looking. They are fair and tall and that increase their self confidence. They rule over the whole world."

Hearing this Gandhi also started eating meat. Gandhi had written about the first experience of eating meat. When he tried mutton for the first time, he felt that the goat was stamping it's feet inside his stomach. He was feeling guilty for hiding this practice of eating meat as his house was strictly following vegetarian meal.

Non vegetarian food is considered as against Hindu customs and their household never use to allow anybody consume meat. Gandhi stopped eating meat as he didn't want to lie to his mother !

In the same way he stopped his habit of smoking also. He also had tried some pranks in his teen age as any other,but he was brave enough to admit his mistakes and ask pardon from his parents.

Once his cousin persuaded him to steal some money from their servant. Later,Gandhi felt so guilty of stealing and tried to commit suicide by eating Datura seeds. Fortunately he survived the attempt as the amount of Datura seeds which he consumed was not enough to die!

Gandhi had narrated about an important and heartrending incident happened when he was 15 years of age. He stole a piece of gold from home for paying off the debt which his brother and friends made by purchasing cigarettes. He knew that stealing is a heinous crime and he was deeply hurt by guilt. He decided to admit his mistake and ask pardon from his Father who was bedridden.

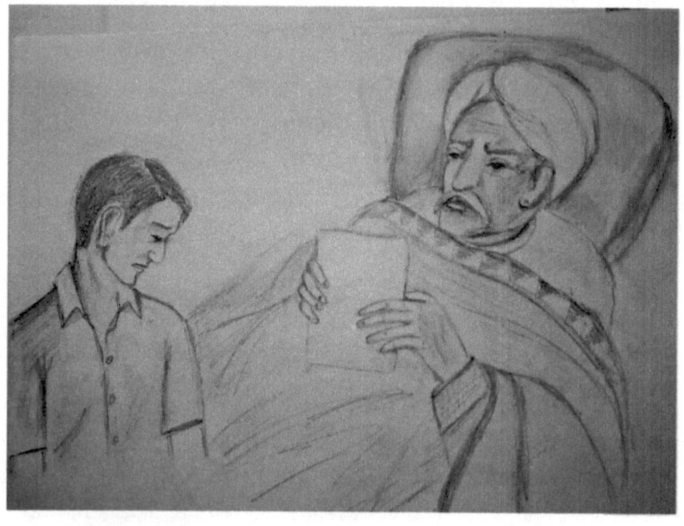

He took a sheet of paper and wrote a letter about what he had done and went to his Fathers room. His father who was lying down,saw Gandhi in his room and got up and sat leaning on the pillows. Gandhi looked at his father who was very tired. Gandhi handed over the sheet of paper in which he had written his confession and stood little far from the bed.

Karam Chand Gandhi took the letter and slowly started reading. Gandhi observed his change of expression and expected an outburst and prepared himself for it. After reading the letter, his Father didn't say a word,but silently tore the paper into bits and put it down.He closed his tear filled eyes and fell back on the cot without even looking at his son. Gandhi could feel the agony on his face and that expression shattered Gandhi.

Gandhi wailed silently. He realised that this is the ultimate punishment. The punishment of non-violence.He took an oath in his mind that here after he will never ever indulge in any kind of wrong doings.

His father taught him the ultimate essence of non-violence. Later Gandhi never left him alone .He was always present next to his bed . He was at his service day and night, looking after him till his death in the year of 1885.!

Chapter - 4: Kasturba Ghandhi

"It is better in prayer to have a heart without words, than words without a heart."

Mahatma Gandhi

Gandhi got married in 1883 at the age of thirteen. Those days child marriage was very common.

Later, in the course of time Gandhi spoke against child marriage and now it is unlawful and banned. More over, now people also aware that, it is wrong to force children into marriage those who have not attained mental and physical maturity.

Those days, elders seek child marriages to strengthen family relations as well as to hold them from going astray when they grow up. Parents decide and execute marriages when they reach twelve or thirteen years of age, according to their will and wish. But children are allowed to continue in their respective homes till they reach a point when they understand about a family life together. Or else they can live in the husband's house as childhood play mates.

Some times if the bridegroom dies,the bride was forced to live as a widow for the rest of her life. A widow who had not even realised what had happened in her life!

Gandhi's marriage also was decided by his parents. One day when Gandhi returned from school,elders of the family talked to him about his marriage.

On the day of his marriage, they dressed him up with beautiful ceremonial dress and took him to Kasturba's house. Kasturba was the daughter of a business man named Gokul Das Makhanji.

Gandhi saw Kasturba sitting on a couch all dressed up in a silk saree and ornaments .He was surprised to see her but fascinated. He kept looking at her with curiosity. She was one year older than Gandhi. After the marriage ceremony,when they returned home with the bride, Gandhi couldn't hide his happiness and surprise that, he got a playmate for himself.

When Kasturba came home,Gandhi felt that he has to take all the responsibility of her and he tried to become the master of her which irked her.

He wanted to educate her as she was illiterate and started tuition classes for her. She,on the other hand didn't like the idea of studying but showed interest in cooking and other house hold chorus. Her negligence towards studies, her behaviour and attitude, altogether irritated Mohan Das. He loved her so much,but at the same time he sought obedience and insisted on seeking permission from him for everything!

Kasturba disagreed with all these restrictions and protested about such behaviour of Gandhi . Thus,after hardly six months of their marriage Kasturba's parents took her home. Gandhi realised that trying to become a "husband" he lost one year of studies.He understood that his false thinking and male chauvinism was wrong.

Then they brought her back home. During these years of growth, Mohan das was undergoing emotional changes in his personality.

In 1887 Gandhi passed matriculation. Though Gandhi had written about him as an average student,if you look at it,out of thirty eight students appeared for matriculation exam only two students had been cleared the exam. Among the two one was Gandhi!

After that he joined Samaldas college in Bhavnagar. Gandhi didn't like the method of education there.Gandhi observed that,students are asked to learn what ever they teach rather than including the students also to be a part of it.

After a period of ten days Gandhi returned home. But for his surprise his brother and friends kept a good news for him that they made arrangements for him to study in London! He always wanted to become a barrister!

His mother Putlibai was worried for two reasons. One was the financial crunch,and the other concern was that her son might eat meat and end up in the company of bad people. The very thought was killing her.Nobody will be there to correct him. At last she took him to a Jain Monk named Becharji Maharaj and made him take an oath that he will follow all the rules and rituals of their cast.

In 1888 September he started his voyage from Madras. Meanwhile his first son Hari Lal was born. He had his first child at the age of sixteen,but the child had survived only a few days. Gandhi was feeling sad to leave his mother, wife and child and also brothers.

Gandhi manged to dress up like the people of London. He dressed up in pants and shirt and wore a tie and an over coat. Though he was feeling very uncomfortable in those outfits, when he looked at himself in the mirror in the ship he felt confident to present himself.

In spite of dressing up like one among them, he was still not confident enough to mingle with the high profile passengers in the ship. He spent his time more in his room reading.

When he alighted from the ship,he observed that others were wearing black coat and hat,where as he was in white flannel clothes. Somehow he managed to reach his hotel. The stay was arranged in Victoria Hotel.

One Dr. Mehta who was Gandhi's well wisher and friend taught him about the different type of outfits in different seasons. While talking Dr Mehta's cap caught his attention which was so beautiful and Gandhi reached for it and touched it.

Mehta immediately corrected Gandhi that he is not supposed to touch other's things and belongings.

"Never touch other's things, never be so inquisitive to ask personal questions. Do not talk loudly or with lot of hand gestures which are the general European etiquette to follow."

Gandhi bought clothes like the people of Landon were wearing. He learn to wear a tie always. He tried to learn dance,but it was not for him. He took the best effort to learn violin,but he couldn't. He spent hours together to take a centre partition and comb his hair and tried to become an English man from every angle.

But inside he wanted to become an Indian. Eventually he became frustrated with all those false prejudices to disguise himself and adapt as an English man.

He realised that there are gaping differences in the culture of both the countries. He hesitated to go to the common dinner hall as he was not comfortable to have only vegetarian food among others who consumed meat and drank wine. He thought that others may notice him.

But later, he himself came to a conclusion that all those habits doesn't matter and he decided to put an end to a life of not his own. A time will come when we realise the foolishness of raking our head about what others think about us though it is not important at all!

He shifted to a room where he cooked for himself and started living like a completely independent Indian. He started wearing Indian clothes in which he is more comfortable and went walking everywhere.He concentrated in his studies. He became a complete vegetarian and wrote articles on the advantages of vegan food. He became the secretory of vegetarian movement!

As there was ample time left for the barrister examination,he decided to take up Landon matriculation also. He studied French,Latin and improved English.

He passed matriculation and every language except Latin. In 1890 Gandhi went to Paris and came back to continue Law. In 1891 Gandhi passed the Ancient law Institute Inner Temple barrister examination.

After all these achievements also, building up self confidence was a challenge.When he reads books of Law several doubts will arise in his head and always doubted about his capability of practicing law. He came back to Rajkot in the same year.

When he came back,a very sad news was waiting for him. His mother who brought him up and made him promise not to forget his birth and culture was no more!

A heart broken Gandhi was informed that soon after he left to Landon she passed away. But they kept the news from Gandhi in the good intention that his studies should not be affected.

Gandhi grieved her death very much!

Chapter - 5: South African Chapter

"An ounce of practice is worth a thousand words."

- *Mahatma Gandhi*

When Gandhi came back as a barrister,his brother and others expected him to become a famous lawyer and earn a fortune out of it. But Gandhi faced a tough competition from the local lawyers who studied locally.They were taking up cases for a very minimal fees and Gandhi who had a Landon degree didn't get any cases.

He felt the barrister degree from Landon was of no worth.Then few of his friends suggested to go to Bombay and study Indian law,so that he can take local cases. At last Gandhi got a case for thirty rupees. On the day of the hearing a nervous Gandhi stood up to plead,but he felt giddy,at the very moment he looked up at the Judge!

Gandhi couldn't continue and got out of the court room. He returned the money to the party. Gandhi always was an introvert from school and never showed any ability to address or give a speech in a public gathering.

The incident in the court room destroyed his confidence even more and one can understand the state of mind which Gandhi had gone through when he desperately applied for a teaching job in an English medium school. Having a London degree of law in hand he applied for the teaching job for a meagre salary of five and half pounds. But he didn't get the Job!

He went back to Rajkot and as he had a flair in writing,he took up a job as a clerical assistant to lawyers. There also he didn't like the job in a court under the British political agent.

Then,as a blessing in disguise,he got a call from South Africa to attend a case of an Indian who was the relative of a known Indian Dada Abdhulla who was settled in South Africa.

That call and invitation changed the history of India as well as Gandhiji's life also.!

Gandhiji along with his wife Kasturba and his two sons, Hari Lal and Mani Lal started from Madras to South Africa by ship in 1893 April 23rd.

He became the legal council of the relative of Dada Abdulla in a place called Transvaal. Though he went to attend the case, the state of Indians in South Africa caught his attention. The condition of Indians were pathetic as the colour prejudice was brutal.

In the month of June Gandhi was directed to travel to Pretoria, [Transvaal] by rail from Natal Durban. This will take him to Pietermaritzburg and from there he had to proceed. Gandhiji purchased one first class ticket and sat in the first class. After sometime one European got into the same compartment and as soon as he saw Gandhiji sitting there called up the railway personal.

He said to Gandhiji very rudely.

"This first class compartment is only for whites. You, Indian labours have to sit in the van compartment."

Gandhiji didn't oblige. He said boldly.

"I have purchased first class ticket and I have every right to sit in this compartment."

Gandhiji was a totally different person from the timid introvert Mohan das.

When the white threatened Gandhiji that, if he wont get up and go he was ready to use force to throw him out.Gandhiji didn't heed. He sat there without moving.

After that one white police man came and pushed Gandhiji from the train to the platform and threw all his belongings and the train flagged off.

About this incident Gandhiji had written like this.

"It was extremely cold outside. I had an over coat in the luggage. But I didn't want to be humiliated again and sat there shivering with cold. A strong thought came to my mind. Should I go back to India or fight for the rights."

This humiliation was only the tip of an ice burg. This incident is one of the symptom of the sickness of a deep routed colour prejudice.

Then, the next day, he travelled from Charlestown to Johannesburg in Stagecoach. He sat on a box next to the coach man. As the conductor was white he sat inside with other Europeans. Gandhiji tolerated the inconvenience and sat there as his journey was important and somehow he must reach the place.

But after some time the conductor came in to smoke. He ordered Gandhiji to leave the box for him and sit on a dirty gunny bag spread there on the floor. But Gandhiji didn't respond and moved from there either. Conductor started abusing him and beating him. At one point he tried to push him from the running train. Gandhiji didn't return the blows but he didn't leave the place by holding on the pole tightly. Listening to the commotion some whites came in and scolded the conductor.

Gandhiji reached Natal and realised that the life in Natal was far more difficult than the sufferings of the people of Transvaal . The people of Natal was charged exorbitant taxes and they were allowed only to stay in a particular area. They were not allowed to come out after nine at night. Indians were not permitted to walk on the footpath.

One must have the permission from the Attorney to move around at night. One day Gandhiji went for a stroll with the no objection letter from the Attorney.

When he reached the lane of president Kruger the security stopped him. The security saw that he was not white and he pushed him from the foot path. When Gandhiji resisted he started beating him on the road.

One Mr. Koats saw this and rushed to the spot as Gandhiji was known to him. He shouted at the security and advised Gandhiji to file a case against him in the Police for this cowardly act.

But Gandhiji decided not to take the matter forward. But Gandhiji was determined to fight for their rights.

When he was in Pretoria he read almost eighty religious literature. Bible influenced him so much which teaches about love and the ultimate sacrifice for i.He regularly attended Bible classes, but never intent to convert. He realised that almost all religion teaches the same lesson of love.

Shortly, Gandhi addressed a huge gathering and spoke about their rights against unlawful discrimination, colour prejudice and racism. He narrated his first class travel experience also. Gandhiji urged the people to stand up for their rights unitedly. He became successful in gathering people from different parts of the country.

He opened a school in Phoenix and introduced wisdom based education. Basic education is the foundation of thought process which brings changes. Gandhiji taught them to fight through "Sathyagraha". The word sathyagraha means Truth force. The army of Truth!. Gandhiji believed in it.

Gandhiji managed to buy one farm in South Africa named Tolstoy farm as his law practice earned good money. Gandhiji gathered people from different parts of the country and encouraged community living. He used the farm for this purpose. According to Gandhi,when you live in a community you never feel to amass wealth independently.

More over that farm was used to give shelter for the family members of those freedom fighters who were jailed. They were looked after by them without any trouble. Gandhiji recruited volunteers and trained them to do service for others including whites if they need any help.

In fact in 1894, Gandhiji had decided to return to India after completing the work in Pretoria. But when Gandhiji wass attending a send off dinner,a very bad news came in.

The South African Government passed a bill which legally approving the discrimination towards Indians. Gandhiji labelled the bill as the "last nail on the coffin".

People urged Gandhiji to cancel his journey and stay for one more month,so that the bill can be challenged in the court. He agreed.

That "one month" stay became twenty long years in South Africa fighting for the freedom of them.

By 1896 Gandhiji became the political leader in South Africa!

During these years till 1913 Gandhiji had undergone several hard ships in the fight for the rights and freedom. He suffered many setbacks as well as success.

Natal formed self Governance and in 1914 the Indian relief bill has been passed and scrapped the tax system.

General Smuts agreed to discuss about other demands and released Gandhiji from Jail.

Gandhiji presented a pair of sandals to General Smuts which he made when he was in Jail. Later, after 25 years General Smuts wrote like this.

"Many a summer I am wearing this pair of sandals made by this great man,well aware that, I am not worthy to wear it."

Gandhiji was happy and satisfied about his work in South Africa and decided to return to India with family through England. The first world war broke out during this period and Gandhiji wanted to help the Indian soldiers under British army.

Meanwhile Mr. Gopala Krishna Gokhale kept informing Gandhiji about the deteriorating situation in India. He used to help Gandhiji in the freedom struggle of South Africa indirectly by funding him financially. He visited Gandhiji and urged him to come back to India as India needs him at this hour of struggle.

Gopala Krishna Gokhale was the leader of Indian national Congress which indulge in many activities in the freedom movement of the country. When Gandhiji returned to India the Indian National Congress gave a grand welcome to Gandhiji. He directed Gandhiji to join the "servant of India society."

When Gandhiji visited Santhi Nikethan he met the Nobel Laurette of 1913, Sri Rabindra Natha Tagore, he addressed Gandhiji "Mahatma"!

Unfortunately Gokhale passed away suddenly. Gandhiji was shocked in the death of his 'guide' as he referd Gokhale and took over the leadership of Congress. Gandhiji mourned Gokhale's death by deciding to walk without using any footwear for one year!

Chapter - 6: Children And "Bapu"

"If we are to teach real peace in the world ...we shall have to begin with the children."

-Mahatma Gandhi

When Gandhiji returned from Johannesburg he decided to travel all over India to get a direct account of their sufferings. He was so fond of children and wherever he goes he will be surrounded by children. It gave him a special enthusiasm. He advised them about the importance of upholding and keeping the promise they take.

An incident may be recalled about a punishment which Gandhiji gave to his second son Mani Lal for not keeping his promise.

Gandhiji was practicing law in the supreme court of Johannesburg. His colleague one Mr. Henry Poluk requested Mani Lal to get one book from the office. The distance from the house to the office were three miles. Mani Lal totally forgot about this. It was quite natural for a thirteen years old kid to forget something which was told.

When Mr. Polak came he enquired about the book. Gandhiji immediately called Mani Lal and asked about the lapse. He said that he forgot to get it.

Gandhiji said.

"When you promise something there is no room for an excuse. You are not suppose to tell any meaningless words. When you take up some matter it must be an oath and you must fulfil it. Now,go and get the book from the office."

Everybody was shocked and stunned as it was already dark and the child has to cover a distance of six miles up and down through an un inhabitant place! Gandhiji also knew that.

Suddenly Mr. Poluck said.

"I can get it tomorrow. Please do not bother. "

Kalyan Bhai also intervened.

"The book can be collected tomorrow also. He is a small child.It is not advisable to send the child at this hour of night. If it is so urgent I will go and get it.

Gandhiji was adamant and said to Kalyan Bhai

"Mani Lal made the promise.Not you. "

At last Mani Lal agreed. But Kalyan Bhai said.

Then let Mani Lal go, but I can accompany him.

Though Gandhiji was comparatively a calm person,he will stick to his decisions like a rock. Kalyan Bhai stepped out in darkness with Mani Lal.

One would be surprised about this punishment as Gandhiji,himself in his childhood dreaded darkness and was afraid to go from one room to the other alone.

But Gandhiji had realised that he became timid and introvert only because he was fearful for many unwanted and unrealistic things. He didn't want his next generation to be like that. More over he wanted to teach him the importance of keeping promises without fail!

Gandhiji started travelling and called upon people by arranging public gathering and urged them to fight for freedom peacefully,

As he was so fond of children,they use to come to him fearlessly. Gandhiji use to answer all the queries whether it is of any importance or otherwise. Once when Gandhiji was attending a meeting one child came up to meet him.

He had come with great expectations to see Gandhiji,as his parents and other people always talked about him. The child looked at the great hero who was a frail small man, in a single piece Dothi. The child was disappointed as he had a different picture in his mind.

He was wondering about his appearance about whom his parents were talking with reverence. He stood there looking at him for some time. In fact he was sympathetic about Gandhiji and came near and asked him.

"Bapuji,why are you not wearing a kurta?"

Gandhiji was taken aback and surprised at the innocence of the child. He smiled at him and said.

"I have no money to buy a kurta my child."

The child was even more surprised that such a great man had no money to buy a kurta. He said.

"My mother stiches beautiful kurtas. I will tell my mother to make one kurta for you."

Gandhiji heard his innocent statement and asked him.

"Okay.., How many kurtas your mother can stich?"

"She can stich how many ever kurtas you need. Two or three?"

"Oh …That may be insufficient. I have a huge family. There…, I have 40 crores of brothers and sisters. I have to give kurtas to all of them and then wear one for myself"!

The child didn't understand what he said, but listened to his statement in surprise with wide opened eyes!

Gandhiji was leading a very normal life and abandoned all foreign goods. He abandoned foreign clothes and started wearing a simple piece of cloth and a small piece of cloth to cover himself. He stopped eating tasty foods and practiced only a simple meal cooked without oil or sault and spices. He has taken into consideration of an average Indian's life and tried to live like one of them.

Gandhiji was saddened as he realised that, in the poverty stricken India a major part of the population are starving. But still the people are innocent, honest and trustworthy to their British masters though they forced them into slavery.

Gandhiji practiced to control his body and mind in order to reach his ultimate aim.

Gandhiji gave importance to certain sentiments which others felt unimportant and silly. Once Gandhiji was attending a congress in Bombay.

Gandhiji was found searching for something under the table and down on the corner.

Kakka Sab Kalekar saw this and asked.

"What are you searching..sir?"

"I cant find my pencil." Gandhiji replied. Without lifting his head. He showed his finger and said.

"The pencil is only so much"

"Oh Is that the matter. I will give you a pencil."

"No. I want to get my pencil which I lost."

In fact Kakka Sab was annoyed. In the midst of such an important meeting Gandhiji was wasting time to search for a small pencil.

Kakkaa sab requested him again but he didn't budge. Then as he knows the determination of Gandhiji even for a small thing,Kakka saab left his futile attempt to convince Gandhi to use some other pencil. He joined hands with him to search the lost pencil.

At last Gandhiji found the pencil from under the table and jumped up with that. He had a child like innocence in his smile when he lifted the pencil. Kakka Sab controlled his laughter as he noticed that the pencil was of hardly two inches long.

Gandhiji said.

"This is not a pencil. This is the love of a child. In Madras Natesan's son pesented me this pencil. Children's love is so important."

Chapter – 7: Gandhiji In Kerala

" The best way to find yourself is to lose yourself in the Service of others."

-Mahatma Gandhi

Gandhi visited Kerala five times. Under British rule, Kerala was divided into three regions. Thiruvithamkur, Malabar and Kochi.

Thiru-Kochi was merged with Madras Province.

From 18th century itself warriors like the famous king Pazhasi raja and other kings and queen fought against British. But,British with their advanced weapons defeated every attempt of the local kings. Gandhiji was the one who changed the whole idea of freedom struggle with his weapon which was 'ahimsa."

Gandhiji has written about the sacrifice of a small girl when he visited Kerala in 1934. He has written an article under the heading "Kaumudi ki thyag "in a Hindi journal . In 1934,Gandhiji visited Kerala and went around places from January 10th to 22nd.

On January 13th In a place called Vatakara, Gandhiji was addressing a public gathering. He expressed his concern over the financial crunch the freedom movement was facing. He emphasized the need for financial assistance from people who can afford to help the poor and the downtrodden.

Gandhiji stopped his speech and people started giving him donations. Suddenly a girl who may be in her teens,boldly came up to the stage and stood smiling before Gandhiji. She removed her gold bangle and gave it to him. Gandhiji was surprised and looked around for her parents.

He stretched his hands to take the bangle from the girl who requested an autograph from the great man. As Gandhiji was putting his signature in her book she removed her other bangle and necklace and gave it to him!

Gandhiji stopped her and said.

This bangle will do and thank you for your generosity. Please do not remove your necklace.

But she surprised him by removing even her ear rings and handed over to him and said.

Here after I will never wear gold jewellery !.

This really moved Gandhiji and he wrote about this great sacrifice which one small girl did for her country.

Gandhiji visited Kerala in 1920 for the first time. He came by train through Madras to Calicut. There he held a meeting of around 500 volunteers.The next day he addressed one public gathering on Calicut beach. The enormous crowd was estimated as 20,000 people.

The freedom movement leader Sri Madhavan Nair translated the speech in Malayalam language for the people. Gandhiji appreciated his work and the news paper "Mathrubhumi" which he was publishing.

The whole country was agitating against the Rowlatt Act. It was a bill passed by the British which allowed any punishment for the arrested freedom prisoners without even a hearing or trial. The verdict cannot be challenged.

Gandhiji's next weapon was non-cooperation movement against this. Gandhiji urged to Boycott foreign goods and the movement became very popular as people burned foreign clothes and joined the movement.

He visited Kerala again when the cast system and untouchability was at its peak. The low casts were not allowed in Temples. They were not even allowed to walk on the pathway to the Temple. The pathway was also divided as "Raja veedhi" and grama veedi [village road].

The "Sathyagraha " in Vaikom was significant and Gandhiji expressed his solidarity for it. Gandhiji insisted the abandonment of cast system and untouchability and he directed the Temple authority to abolish the law and allow everybody to enter into the temple.

"All are equal in front of God!" He said.

He visited Sri Narayana Guru In an Asram situated in Varkkala,who was working on the movement named "entry to the temple for all"

The next visit was to Trissur Vivekodayam school where he encouraged every body to use khadi clothes spinning in charka locally to promote native clothes.There,they had arranged one competition in spinning clothes in Charka. In this competition "Mankulam Mallika thampuraatti " who was the niece of Karur Nila kanta Pillai won. Gandhiji presented her the award!

The great poet Vallathol Narayana Menon visited Gandhiji whom he was considered as a "Guru." Vallaththol called the visit as the Master student meeting!

The fourth visit was with Kasturba Gandhi and they reached Palghat Shornur in 1934.January. Gandhiji witnessed the successful Temple entry for the Dalits and Kaimadham Ayyappa temple was opened for Dalits. It was a landmark victory as the first Temple opened for Dalits in the whole country.

The fifth and final visit was in 1937 January 12th. Gandhiji had written about the journey which lasted till 21st was the happiest and was like a pilgrimage for him. He came to announce the ordinance passed by the King of Thiruvithamkur Sri.'Chithira thirunaal Bala Rama verma that Temple entry is open to all communities.

Gandhiji was so happy and great full to the king. After that he visited Ayyankali who was working for the upliftment of 'Harijans.'

This descriptions are only about Kerala chapter. In the same way Gandhiji travelled all other states and every nook and corner of India to enlighten them about freedom movement.

Gandhiji wrote about his travel like this.

"I travel every where in the beautiful anticipation that every body want to meet me. I need to meet all the people. I speak up my mind to them in limited sentences.I am certain that sooner or later, those words will penetrate their mind!"

Chapter – 8: The Value of a Copper Coin

"Where there is love, there is life!"

- Mahatma Gandhi

Gandhiji led a war of non violence, non co-operation and boycott of foreign goods against the gun and cannons of British. Gandhiji urged people to boycott all foreign goods and follow "Swadeshi movement "

He asked everybody to make their own clothes and taught them the usage of charka to make thread and weave clothes.The picture of a humble frail figure who sits with crossed legs and making cotton threads became a symbol of swadeshi movements. It reminds everybody the struggle of freedom movement and the man behind it. Mahatma Gandhi!

He initiated a charka group in which lot of people joined and they spin thread from cotton and weave clothes in charka. This initiative was in the interest of teaching people to become self oriented and self sufficient.

Gandhiji wanted to spread the awareness among people. As there was no means of communication like present day, he visited many places and donated charka.He taught people how to use it and urged them to make their own clothes inorder to abandon foreign clothes.

There was a lot of expenditure for making and distributing charka and seeking for donations became inevitable. People were so generous and helped the movement by extending monetory help.

A person named Jaman Lal Bajaj kept the accounts and entered in a ledger about all the donations in gold and money .Once Gandhiji was talking in a meeting in Orissa,one very old lady stood up from the crowd. She was wearing torn clothes and stooped because of old age. The volunteers tried to make her sit but she didn't budge.

She was determined and adamant that she must go near Gandhiji and meet him. At last the volunteers agreed reluctantly. Some how she made her way to Gandhiji and bowed in front of him to touch his feet. Then she took one copper coin which was kept in the folding of her saree very carefully and placed it at the feet of Gandhiji. After that she walked away silently with her wavering steps.

Tears filled in Gandhiji's eyes as he took the copper coin in his hands. Gandhiji was surprised .He thought,that is not a coin but the love and generosity of a common poor lady! Later when Jaman Lal asked for the copper coin to account it,Gandhiji didn't give it to him.

Jaman Lal mocked and expressed his mind.

"Bapu,I am keeping thousands of rupees and cheques safely. But you have no trust to hand over this copper coin into my custody."?

"But this copper coin is more valuable than all those money. What is great in donating thousand or two thousand rupees from lakhs of money? On the other hand this copper coin is the whole earning of that poor lady who spared it for the freedom struggle. So this coin has more value. Helping mentality is more important than the quantity!

Gandhiji travelled every nook and corner of the country and urged the people about the course of action in the freedom fight. He appreciated even the least initiative and struggle and was ready to correct himself if needed.

Non violent agitation was Gandhiji's weapon and fasting was his trump card. This mode of agitation was Gandhiji 's idea which he started and materialised in South Africa. According to Gandhi "Sathyagraha" was a unique weapon to fight injustice. It was a novel method of mass agitation which stressed the principle of truth,tolerance,non violence and peaceful protests.

In the path of Sathyaagraha,fasting was the toughest mechanism. Go without food or water till the demands are met. Gandhiji fasted several times and the longest was 21 days without food and water. British government came to their knees in front of these fasting agitation of Gandhiji.

British busted any agitation and public gathering. They punished people very severely so that they dare not raise a voice against the British.

One can never forget the Brutal massacre at Jallianwala Bagh on April 13 1919. The public had gathered to celebrate Baisakhi. The British accused it as a political gathering and opened fire at the unarmed civilians,including women,and children.

Gandhiji launched the first nonviolent agitation in the country in Champaran district of Bihar and Kheda district of Gujarat in 1917. The term "Sathyagraha" was first used against the Rowlatt Act.

Rowlatt Act passed in 1919 by the imperial Legislative council authorised the British Government to arrest anybody suspected of terrorist activities.It also authorised the government to detain such people arrested for two years without trial. It empowered the police to search and raid a place without warrant!

Whenever the freedom movement catches up and agitating people from all over the country unite,the British will charge false case on the leaders and shut them in jail.

Indian revolutionaries were deported to Andaman islands and jailed in the cellular jail, the infamous "kalapani" As the freedom movement in India continued to grow the British housed the political prisoners in it and meted them with rigorous

torture.Frequent executions took place in full view of the cells.After a campaign by Mahatma Gandhi and Rabindra Natath Tagore prisoners from the cellular jail were sent back.

Gandhiji was imprisoned almost thirteen times in South Africa and India. Gandhiji made use of his jail term for writing. He wrote letters and pamphlets to the leaders outside. He wrote many articles when he was in jail.

Once,Gandhiji was arrested for publishing three of his articles in "Young India."

He was picked up from Sabarmati Ashram in March 1922 and sentenced for nine years. Later after two years he was released unconditionally from Yerwada Jail.

There were some interesting stories which Sardar Vallabhai Patel and Gandhiji told each other when they were imprisoned in Yerwada Jail. The stories were appropriate for the occasion. Gandhiji said.

"Sometimes a dead snake Is also useful. Once a snake sneaked into one old lady's house. She screamed for help and neighbours came and killed the snake. They flung the dead snake to the roof. One eagle was flying past with an expensive pearl necklace on its beak and happened to see the dead snake on the top of the house. The eagle dropped the pearl necklace for the dead snake as it was it's food The old lady found something shining on the top of her house and was very happy when she realised that it was an expensive necklace which was a fortune for her. "

Listening to this Saradar Patel told one story.

" Once one snake sneaked into a "Baniya's" house. He didn't want to kill the snake as he believed in non violence. He believed that killing is sin. He was reluctant to call for help also. He covered the curled up snake with a mud pot and went to sleep thinking that he may call somebody for help the next day.

That night a thief came to that house and saw the mud pot kept upside down. The thief thought the house owner must have kept some valuables under it and lifted the mud pot only for a shock of his life. The snake hissed and bit him and he ran for his life."

Patel told this story as Gandhiji was from 'Baniya ' religion and his mode of operandi was nonviolence.

The remarkable scrutiny and efficiency of Gandhiji was exceptional and he expected the same from others also. Manu Gandhi's punishment may be a clear example for this. Manu Gandhi and Abha Gandhi were taking care of Gandhiji's personal matters. Manu was Gandhiji's cousin sister's grand daughter.

Restless life and many fasting took a toll on Gandhiji 's health.Manu Gandhi and Abha Gandhi were the supporting staff of Gandhiji who use to walk by hanging on the shoulders of these girls on both the sides.

Gandhiji was travelling everywhere to console and compromise people during the post independence agitation among Hindus and Muslims. Gandhiji reached every village by foot. He starts in the morning from one village and reached another by sun set. A tired Gandhiji took bath as soon as he reaches the other village.

Once,when he reached a village in Nokkali,Manu Gandhi kept water for Gandhi's bath and suddenly realised that the pumice stone which he uses for scrubbing his feet was missing. She searched for it and didn't find.

She reported it to Gandhiji.

"Bapu,the pumice stone is missing. We must have misplaced it in the weaver's village where we stayed yesterday. "Now what shall I do?"

Bapu answered. "Oh is it so. Then go get it from there"!

Manu was shocked. The previous day they stayed in a faraway village. Now Gandhi demands to get it she has to walk a long way through farm lands, coconut tree plantations and forest. Possibilities are there to get lost also. At last she asked.

"Let me take somebody along with me." Bapu replied.

"Why? You go alone. This kind of carelessness must not be repeated."

Manu was hardly sixteen years of age and had not gone anywhere alone. But she didn't want to admit that she was afraid to go alone.

At last Manu started alone. She followed the footsteps and reached the weaver's village tired and worn out. The old lady of the village recognised her right away and asked her what happened.

Manu told her about the missing stone. But unfortunately little she knew about the importance of the stone and the old lady threw the stone along with other trash!

Manu was disappointed but started searching for it. The old lady also joined and after searching for a long time they found the stone.

Manu returned with the stone covering miles by walk. She reached back by running and walking and handed over the pumice stone to Gandhiji and bursted into tears.

Gandhiji consoled her.

"This stone was a testing time for you. You must not be careless. Meeraben gave me this stone twenty five years back. This stone was with me during all my journeys and in palace as well as in Jail. You should not be a cause to loose this stone. This was a test even for me also.

Women must be brave,independent and self sufficient. !

Chapter – 9: Independence

"Freedom is not worth having if it does not include the Freedom to make mistakes."

– Mahatma Gandhi.

"A nation's culture resides in the hearts and the souls of it's people."

—Mahatma Gandhi.

In 1942,"Quit India " movement started under the leadership of Gandhiji after the all India Congress working committee meeting on August 8.

British must leave India!

British Government had already witnessed the unity in the agitation of "salt Sathyagraha"or "Dandi March ". The Salt Sathyagraha was a mass civil disobedience movement initiated by Mahatma Gandhi against the salt tax imposed by the British Government in India. Gandhiji led a large group of people from Sabarmati Ashram on 12th March 1930 till Dandi, a coastal village in Gujarat,to break the salt law by producing salt from sea water. The distance from Sabarmati Ashram to

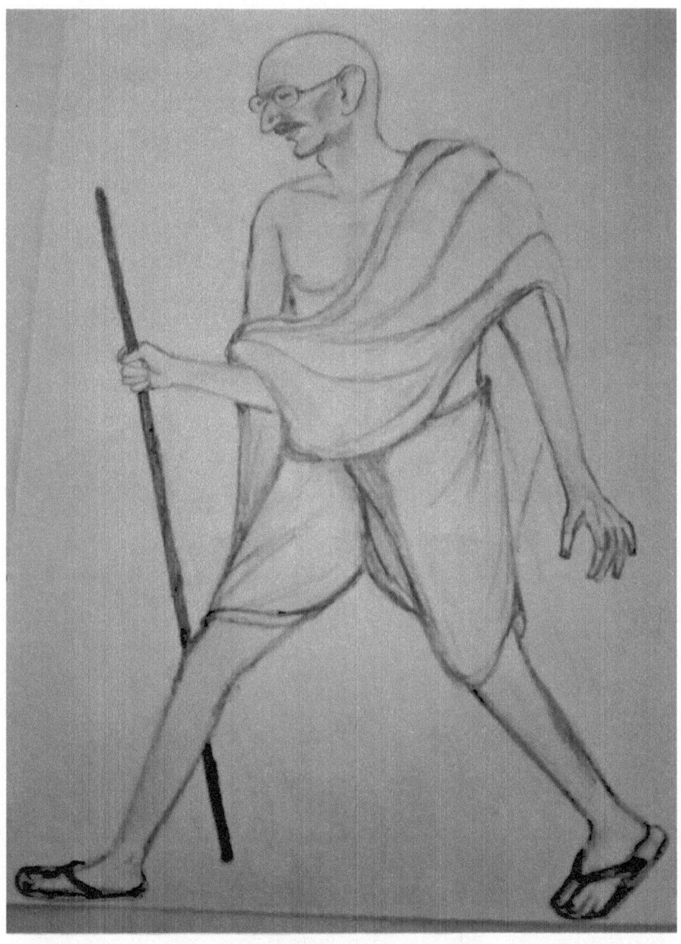

Dandi was 241 miles and they walked for 24 days 10 miles a day. They themselves made salt from sea water.

Gandhiji said,the coast belongs to India and the British imposed heavy tax on the natives for the salt made from the sea. It is unlawful and cannot be tolerated.

After the salt sathyagraha,Quit India movement was the largest mass agitation spread all over India. India was getting closer to freedom."Quit India movement can be described as the last and final agitation in the course of freedom struggle.

Initiating the agitation Gandhiji gave a speech which penetrated every heart.

" Do or die. We shall either free India or die in the attempt, we shall not live to see the perpetuation of slavery".The speech was called for determined but passive resistance,or civil disobedience based on the principle of Sathyagraha. The speech delivered by Gandhiji pushed the cause for Indian Independence from British colonial rule.

But as soon as the Quit India movement started,the British Government arrested Jawahar Lal Nehru and Gandhiji and shut them in Jail. Other important leaders also were imprisoned.

Gopala Krishna Gokhale wrote in Marathi.

"Swaraj is my birth right and I shall have it."

In every way the agitation was spread the whole nation and British Government had no other option, but passed the Indian Independence bill in British Parliament in 1947 and India became free.

In fact British Government was unable to face and supress the agitation in India as it was affected from the second world war. America refused to help Britain during the crisis. British Government was under immense pressure because of the nonstop agitation of the people of India .

In the presence of British Prime minister Mr. Clement Atly and Governor general Lord Mount Batton the bill was passed and it was decided that,by 1948 June, all British people must leave India.

Indian Independence was declared at the midnight hour of August 15, 1947 and Jawahar Lal Nehru became the first prime minister of India. But the agitation among Hindus and Muslims were out of hand and the congress committee also had to agree with the British Government for the demand of partition. It became inevitable and divided India into two nations as Pakistan and India!

The partition has witnessed heartrending scenes along the border as families also parted in the melee. In the chaotic situation people lost their near and dear ones to the other side of the border.

After this,incidents of unrest and agitation in the name of cast was followed and became out of control in the country. Gandhiji was saddened as he sacrificed his entire life for the freedom of his country,but the turn out was unexpected.

Gandhiji went into fasting and declared that until people stop fighting he will never eat or drink. He told he will fast unto death. At last leaders on both the sides brought back peace and Gandhiji stopped his fasting.

Gandhiji began to travel the whole country and talked to people directly to bring back peace. The independence struggle started in 1857 by the then martyr kings like Pazhassi Raja, Tipu Sultan and queen Jhancy Rani of different provinces. Then at last after years of struggle,when the country attained freedom the internal peace was at stake.

Gandhiji travelled and tried to remove the misunderstandings among the Hindu Muslim brothers,but before he could complete his mission Gandhiji's life was cut short by bullets fired by a radical extremist named Nathuram Godse!

On the fateful day, Gandhiji who was very weak walked with the help of Manu Gandhi and Abha Gandhi to the prayer hall. As he was walking Godse approached him and bowed with folded hands. Then he took his gun and pushed Manu Gandhi aside and fired.

The bullets hit him point blank on his chest, the chest which has only love towards everybody.

[The awestruck and shocked Manu Gandhi's picture with blood stained clothes is exhibited in Gandhi Museum]

No one did realise what had happened. As Gandhiji collapsed and closed his eyes for ever he chanted.,

"He Ram ".

That was the last word came out of the great soul! The word "He Ram " is inscribed in the monument at Raj Ghat

After the funeral Manu Gandhi noted in her diary.

'Till yesterday " Bapu" was with me. Today at least his body was there. But now I became alone,totally lonely!'

The whole country had shed tears in the same thought.

Now we became alone .Totally lonely!!

About the Author

Briji. KT

Bilingual writer and Artist.Published many books including a collection of Poems "Zoetrope" and Historical fiction "Thirteen to Thirty" by Ukiyoto Publishers. Books are publishe by leading publishers like Poorna publishers, Budha books, Saikatham books Red Cherry books, Kerala Gov. Institute for Childrens literature,Telbrain publishers for childrens literature etc.

Won many awards for contribution in literature and art. Nari Ujjagaran award and International Muse award for Poetry, Santha kumaran Thampi award, OV.Vijayan puraskaaram, kairali puraskaaram etc and Women achievers award 2020. In the field of art,conducted several exhibitions and attended national art camps and won awards.

Illustration by .BRIJI.K.T .

www.ingramcontent.com/pod-product-compliance
Lightning Source LLC
Chambersburg PA
CBHW051448140726
47987CB00006B/2605